MW01152868

OUR GREEK AND LATIN ROOTS

James Morwood and Mark Warman

Latin and Ancient Greek were the languages of two great nations some two thousand years ago. People often call these languages 'dead', but they are in fact very much alive. In this book we show the ways in which they still matter to us.

In the first three Units we tell the story of the spread of Latin through Britain and the world. In Unit 4 we show how English words are often built up from Latin. In Unit 5 we trace the history of the Greek language and show how it came to influence English. In Unit 6 we give examples of this influence. Then in Unit 7 we discuss the differences between English and Latin grammar.

We end in Unit 8 with a number of activities which develop things we said earlier. These activities can be tackled at any stage in the book.

1. **The family of Latin languages**

2. **The Romans in Britain**

3. **Our Latin roots**

4. **Building English from Latin**

5. **How Greek entered English**

6. **The Greeks had a word for it**

7. **Latin Grammar and English – same or different?**

8. **et cetera**

CAMBRIDGE UNIVERSITY PRESS

Awareness of Language

Series Editor: Eric Hawkins

The *Awareness of Language* series is an introduction to how language works which will be useful in the context of Modern Languages and/or English teaching. This book is one of several short topic books, each of which covers a particular aspect of language – with a strong emphasis on practical activities involving the pupil. The books may be used one at a time, in any order – together they form a coherent whole covering the main aspects of language awareness.

PUBLISHED BY THE PRESS SYNDICATE OF THE UNIVERSITY OF CAMBRIDGE
The Pitt Building, Trumpington Street, Cambridge CB2 1RP, United Kingdom

CAMBRIDGE UNIVERSITY PRESS
The Edinburgh Building, Cambridge CB2 2RU, UK http://www.cup.cam.ac.uk
40 West 20th Street, New York, NY 10011–4211, USA http://www.cup.org
10 Stamford Road, Oakleigh, Melbourne 3166, Australia

First published 1990
Fifth printing 1998

Printed in the United Kingdom at the University Press, Cambridge

A catalogue record for this book is available from the British Library

Library of Congress Cataloging in Publication data

Morwood, James.
    Our Greek and Latin roots/James Morwood and Mark Warman.
        p.   cm. – (Awareness of language).
    1. English language – Foreign elements – Greek.   2. English language –
Foreign elements – Latin.   3. Greek language – Influence on English.
4. Latin language – Influence on English.   5. English language –
Word formation.   6. English language – Roots.   I. Warman, M. S.
(Mark S.)   II. Title.   III. Series.
    PE1582.G6M67   1990
    422′.481 – dc20   89-23922
                                                                                        CIP

ISBN 0 521 37841 9

THE FAMILY OF LATIN LANGUAGES

Southern Italy

Latin is often called a 'dead' language. But is it? About a quarter of the world's population still keep Latin alive in their speech. If you find this hard to believe, read on.

To begin with, *Lat*in was spoken in *Lat*ium, an area of central Italy. It was the language of the Romans, who founded their city of Rome in Latium in 753 BC.

If you go to Rome today, you will find copies of this famous statue in every souvenir shop. It shows Romulus, the founder of Rome, and his brother Remus being suckled by a she-wolf. The story goes that the wicked king who had seized control of this part of Italy tried to kill these baby boys. They were said to be the sons of the god Mars and the king did not want them to grow up and take his throne from him. They were left out on the banks of the river Tiber to be swept away in its waters. But a kindly she-wolf rescued them and made sure that they survived.

- Why do you think that the city which Romulus founded was called Rome?

- The word 'martial' comes from the name Mars. What does it mean? What are martial arts?

- And so what was Mars the god of?

- How else has his name survived in the modern world?

- What can we tell about the Romans' attitude to life from the fact that they imagined Mars to be their ancestor?

The power of this warlike people gradually spread throughout the whole of Italy. The different tribes in Italy each had their own language, but Latin became the dominant language because it was spoken by the ruling tribe.

This book is written in English, but in London, England, 160 different languages are spoken, and in the USA and Canada over 100 languages are used for instruction in schools in different parts of the country. How many different languages are spoken by the people in your school or college? What are they?

Would it be better if everyone in your country spoke only English? Write out a list of ways in which it would be better. Then write out a list of ways in which it would be worse. Which side do you agree with?

THE SPREAD OF LATIN

By the end of the first century B.C., the Romans had built up a great empire outside Italy. They had conquered almost all of Europe and all the countries around the Mediterranean.

Write down the modern names of ten of the countries, cities or rivers on the map opposite. Sometimes the Roman names are exactly the same as the modern names.

Can you work out from the following why the Mediterranean Sea was given its name?

medium	*territory*	(What do these two words mean?)
medius	*terra*	(Latin words)
middle	*land*	(English meanings)

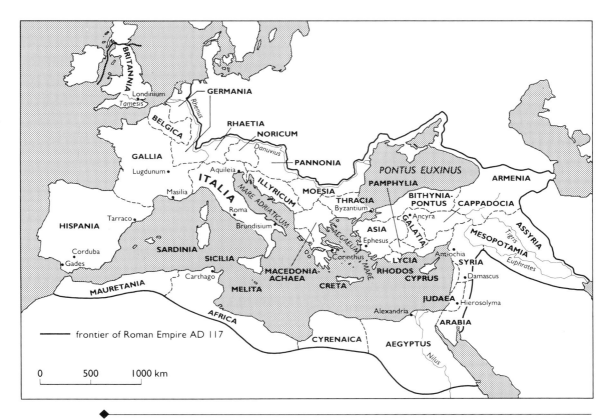

THE ROMANCE LANGUAGES

Latin became the language of educated people in the Western countries of the Roman Empire. In the countries where the Romans had been longest, their language grew deep roots. The languages used today in Spain, Italy, France, Portugal and Romania are directly descended from Latin. You can see how Latin has influenced these languages by looking at the words for the numbers 1–10.

	Latin	Italian	Spanish	French	Portuguese	Romanian
1	unus	uno	uno	un	um	un
2	duo	due	dos	deux	dois	doi
3	tres	tre	tres	trois	três	trei
4	quattuor	quattro	cuatro	quatre	quarto	patru
5	quinque	cinque	cinco	cinq	cinco	cinci
6	sex	sei	seis	six	seis	șase
7	septem	sette	siete	sept	sete	șapte
8	octo	otto	ocho	huit	oito	opt
9	novem	nove	nueve	neuf	nove	noua
10	decem	dieci	diez	dix	dez	zece

Imagine that you belong to a sports team playing for Ancient Rome. (You can choose the sport, but remember that none of the scores may be above ten.) Challenge three modern countries from the list above to play against you, and give the scores in the native language of each team. Yours, of course, will always be in Latin. Get a friend to put these scores into English.

Look at these words for 'five': *cinque* (Italian), *cinq* (French), *fünf* (German), *five* (English), *cinco* (Spanish), *fem* (Danish). Which of them do *not* come from Latin?

What is the reason for the names of our last four months? (Note: The first month of the Roman year was March.)

We call Italian, Spanish, French, Portuguese and Romanian 'Romance' languages because they were originally spoken by the Romans. The word 'romance' also has other meanings which developed over time in three stages:
1. It was used to describe stories written in one of these languages about knights and their adventures.
2. This led to its meaning any story full of wonderful and extraordinary happenings.
3. From that it came to mean the sort of book which deals with love in a sentimental way, or simply to mean a love affair itself.

The Romance languages developed more from the Latin spoken by ordinary people than from the grand Latin of the Empire builders – which even many native Romans found difficult! The Latin word for ordinary people is *vulgus*. So we call the language from which the Romance languages grew 'Vulgar Latin'.

What does the word 'vulgar' mean today? Think of some things which you consider vulgar. Do you think it is fair to link them with 'ordinary people'?

There are in fact two separate meanings of the word 'vulgar'. What are they?

In 'educated' Latin the word for a horse was *equus*. Can you think of any English words derived from this? In Vulgar Latin, the word for a horse was *caballus*. In Spanish this turned into *caballo*, and in Italian into *cavallo*. In French it became *cheval*. Which English words to do with horses and the people who ride them have come from *caballus*? What does chivalry, which comes from *cheval*, have to do with a horse?

You can see that some words changed their spellings as they moved from Latin to another language:

Latin	French	English
caballus	cheval	chivalry
taberna	taverne	tavern
mercator	marchand	merchant
cantus	chant	chant

THE ROMANCE LANGUAGES SPREAD

Many centuries after the Roman Empire had fallen, the Romance-speaking Spaniards and Portuguese colonized huge areas of the world. See if you can find out where and when. They took their Latinate languages with them and as a result these are now spoken by many millions of people outside Europe.

Match up the name of each country with the correct number. Which of these countries were colonized by the Spaniards and which by the Portuguese?

ARGENTINA
BOLIVIA
BRAZIL
CHILE
COLUMBIA
ECUADOR
GUYANA
GUYANE
PARAGUAY
PERU
SURINAM
URUGUAY
VENEZUELA

> **Some facts**
> 1. Spanish is the national language of 19 countries (mainly in South America).
> 2. Spain has 33 million Spanish native speakers (plus some 4 millions of bilingual Catalans, Basques and Galicians who speak Spanish as their second language).
> 3. The total number of Spanish native speakers in the world is about 280 millions (including some 12 million Spanish native speakers in the USA).
> 4. Portugal has 10 million native speakers of Portuguese. There are more than 150 million Portuguese native speakers in the world.
> 5. In one South American country alone there are some 120 million native speakers of Portuguese. Which country is this?
>   (Answer below.)

Here are some Spanish and Portuguese words with the Latin words which they come from. See if you can find out what they mean in English:

Spanish	Portuguese	Latin
amigo	amigo	amicus
gato	gato	cattus
libertad	liberdade	libertas
vela	vela	velum
arte	arte	ars
carne	carne	caro

Have another look at the map of South America. You will see that Spanish and Portuguese are spoken over a huge area. Why do you think that the whole area has become known as Latin America?

Where else is Spanish spoken – and why?

Look again at the first paragraph at the beginning of this Unit. Do you believe that statement now? Or do you have any doubts about it, and if so what are they?

> The Latin language was always open to influences from outside Rome. Most of the great writers who shaped the Latin language did not come from Rome itself. The famous public speaker Cicero was born 70 miles from Rome. This may seem a short distance, but a proud Roman nobleman called him an immigrant. Seneca, a philosopher and playwright who taught the Roman Emperor Nero, came from Cordoba in Spain.
>
> Latin belongs to millions of people, not just a privileged few.

2 · THE ROMANS IN BRITAIN

When Julius Caesar invaded Britain in 55 and 54 B.C., he raided the country but did not conquer it.

CAESAR

KAISER   CZAR

Julius Caesar was an individual, but what did the word 'Caesar' come to mean? (Note: in Latin *c* was pronounced with the sound *k* in all words.) Which country was ruled by the Kaiser, and which by the Czar?

Julius Caesar and his adopted son Augustus gave their names to the months of July and August.

Julius Caesar, the Roman general and statesman

Kaiser Wilhelm, the last Emperor of Germany, who led his country to defeat in the First World War

Czar Nicholas, the last Czar of Russia, who was executed in 1918

A hundred years later, in 43 A.D., a general sent out by the Emperor Claudius Caesar carried out a successful conquest and Britain became part of the Roman Empire.

Britain in the first century A.D., showing the main roads and towns.

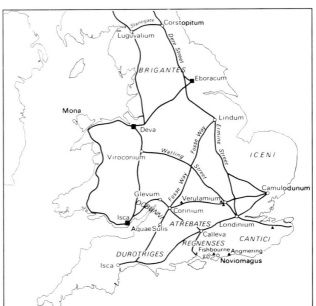

The Romans made a great difference to the way people lived in Britain. The Britons were mainly country people who lived in hut-villages or on isolated farms. Their wealth came from agriculture and the metals which they mined. The Roman way of life, however, was based on towns, which provided centres for markets and trade and for the administration of the laws. So they wanted to establish towns in Britain as well.

If you build towns you need roads to connect them. The Romans were famous for the great network of roads they built throughout their Empire, and they established in Britain many thriving towns linked by first class roads.

What were Roman roads famous for?

The Latin word for a road is *via*. What is a 'viaduct'? In what way is an aqueduct different from a viaduct? 'I went to Chester *via* London.' What does *via* mean in this sentence?

Identify Colchester, Cirencester, Chester and Lancaster. Use an atlas or a road map.

Find out which major roads now link York and London, London and Colchester, Exeter and London.

Roman roads were often raised on an embankment above the countryside they passed through. This is why speakers of Old English called these roads 'highways'.

Roman roads were usually paved. The Latin word for a laid surface is *stratum*. This entered our language as 'straet' and is now 'street'. Remember this the next time you are walking along the High Street.

What does the word 'strata' (the plural of *stratum*) mean today? What has this meaning in common with the surface of a road?

It would have surprised the Romans to know that one day on their roads would move vehicles called Astra, Audi, Carina, Corolla, Cortina, Fiat, Mercedes, Volvo – all Latin words!

> In a letter recently found at a Roman fort in Northumberland, the writer complains, 'I would have fetched the ox hides but I didn't want to cause difficulties for the mules as the roads are bad.' Do you think that he's more likely to be moaning about the potholes or about the travel conditions in winter weather?

> The word 'mile' is from the Latin word *mille* meaning 'thousand'. A mile was a thousand Roman 'paces'. The Roman mile was a bit shorter than ours, 1640 yards as opposed to our 1760.

The Latin word for camp was *castra*. This entered English as 'caester' and became 'cester', 'chester', 'caistor' or 'caster'. Make a list of five places in Britain or North America with one of these words ending their name. You can see that the Romans' camps have become part of the twentieth-century map of the world.

The Roman soldiers (*milites* in Latin) have left us a number of other words. You will have no trouble in giving the English

On tent poles over their left shoulders, these Roman soldiers are carrying a heavy burden of kit, including a pack, a bottle for wine and cooking pots. The total weight could be as much as 60 pounds.

equivalents of these Latin words: *militaris, militia, arma*. The Latin word *salarium* means the 'salt ration' which Roman soldiers were given as their payment. What English word comes from this? They called their kit *impedimenta*. Why?

Many Latin words entered the language which the British then spoke. (It was called Celtic.) Some of these words have survived in Welsh, one of the descendants of Celtic. Compare the Welsh words with the equivalent words in French, Spanish and Italian.

Latin	Welsh	English	French	Spanish	Italian
pons	pont	bridge	pont	puente	ponte
ecclesia	eglwys	church	église	iglesia	chiesa
castra	car, caer	camp, chester	champ	castro	campo
schola	ysgol	school	école	escuela	scuola

> The word *ecclesia*, which the Welsh *eglwys* comes from, was a Greek word before it became a Latin one. This is true of many Latin words – not surprisingly, since educated Romans spoke both Latin and Greek. In their early years, they learned Greek from an educated Greek slave in the household who was employed as a language assistant. Greek was the language which had prestige for the Romans. So where Latin travelled, a bit of Greek and some knowledge of Greek stories and myths went with it.
>
> Is there one particular modern language which English-speakers wish to learn nowadays? If so, which language – and why?

Is there a person of Welsh origin in your class? If so, see how many Welsh place names he or she can think of which include the words *pont, eglwys, car* and *caer*. If not, how many can *you* track down?

The Roman army left Britain near the start of the fifth century A.D. Their Empire was threatened on all sides and it did not seem sensible to defend a cold Northern island.

Make a list of the changes left behind in Britain after the Roman occupation. If you can find a book on the Roman world, you may be able to add some more to the ones mentioned in this book.

3 ◆ OUR LATIN ROOTS

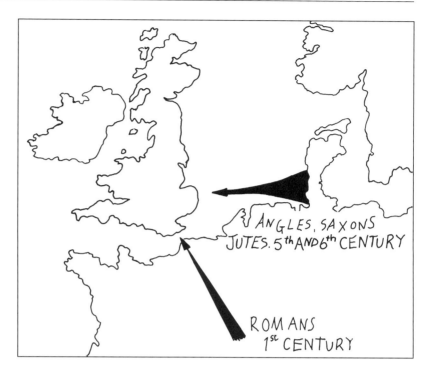

In the fifth and sixth centuries A.D. Britain was invaded by the Saxons, Jutes and Angles, who came from the Netherlands, Northern Germany and Denmark. They brought their own language with them, which was called Anglo-Saxon. This was a Germanic language, from the same family of languages as Latin but only a distant relation. Anglo-Saxon became the leading everyday language of Britain.

Latin, however, was the traditional language of the Christian Church, and, as Christianity spread, so too did its language.

In the sixth century A.D., the future Pope Gregory was one day walking in the market place at Rome when he saw some fair-haired boys from Britain about to be sold as slaves. On being told that they were Angles (*Angli* in Latin), he said that the name was right for them because they had the faces of angels (*angeli*). It was this conversation which inspired St Augustine to go to Britain in 597 A.D. to convert this country to the Christian God. In fact, Christianity was already thriving in various parts of Britain but Augustine's arrival gave it a new momentum – and this spread the Latin language still further.

'Our Father . . .' The Lord's Prayer in Latin

Why was Latin the language of the Church? Rome was the capital of the Christian Church and the home of its Pope (this word came from *Papa*, a Latin word for Father). After the collapse of the Roman Empire in the fifth century A.D., Latin remained the Church's main link with its past. Priests continued to say or sing the services and read the Bible in Latin. Because Latin was still widely understood and was used outside the Church as the language of diplomacy, business and trade, it could help the growth of Christianity.

The New Testament was originally written in Greek. Now it was read in a Latin translation. This translation was called the Vulgate. Why? (Hint: What did the Latin word *vulgus* mean in Unit 1 (p.6)?)

Until fairly recently, Roman Catholic Church services were held in Latin. Now they are almost always conducted in the native language of the country concerned. Make a list of the obvious advantages of this change. Can you think of any good reasons for conducting services in Latin, as still occasionally happens?

You may already know the meaning of *Ave Maria*, *Dies irae*, *Te Deum*, *Requiem*, *Adeste fideles* and *Nunc dimittis*. If not, find out. There's a connection with music too. What is it?

The Latin word *pastor* means 'shepherd'. How does this explain its meaning in English? What does 'pastoral' mean?

Britten's *War Requiem*, composed in 1961, sets to music the Latin mass for the dead together with poems by the great war poet, Wilfred Owen

A major turning-point in the development of English came when the Normans invaded Britain in 1066. French became the language of the new Court, the government, the schools, and the houses of the nobility. Latin stayed the language of the Church as well as the language of international communication. So Latin words now poured into the English language in two ways, through French, and through the Church. There were more than 10,000 of these Latinate words and 75% of them are still being used.

Many of the words borrowed after 1066 from the Latin via French belonged to such groups as:

government	church	law	fighting	learning	medicine
crown	sermon	justice	army	study	doctor
regal	religion	jury	navy	science	patient
minister	service	defendant	military	master	cure

What do you think these groups of words have in common with each other? Why do you think that Latinate words were used for these activities?

Have a look at the following groups of words, the first from Old English, the second from Old French. Can you spot any major difference between the meaning of the words in the two English lists? (Hint: Where did the Normans usually come across these animals?) What does this tell us about the difference between the Normans and the English?

English	Old English
ox	oxa
calf	cealf
sheep	scēap
pig	picga
swine	swīn

English	Old French	Latin
beef	boeuf	bos
veal	veël	
mutton	mouton	
pork	porc	porcus

If it was necessary to use a costly instrument to tell the time, the English words came from the Norman French ('second', 'minute', 'hour', from Latin *secundus*, *minutus*, *hora*). If a costly instrument was not needed, they came from Anglo-Saxon ('day', 'noon', 'week', 'month', 'year', from Anglo-Saxon *daeg*, *nōn*, *wice*, *mōnath*, *geār*). Why do you think this was? Note though that the French and Latin words for day and year (Latin: *dies*, *annus*; French: *jour*, *an*) have given rise to some English words – for example, 'annual' and 'journey'. (By the way, our present calendar of 365 days was first introduced by Julius Caesar.)

Now look at the following two columns of words. The first consists of English words from the Anglo-Saxon (the Anglo-Saxon words given in brackets), the second of English words imported from Latin through French (the Latin words given in brackets):

motherly	(*modor*=mother)	maternal	(*maternus*)
go down	(*gan*=go)	descend	(*descendere*)
drink	(*drincan*)	imbibe	(*imbibere*=drink in)
high	(*heāh*)	elevated	(*elevare*=lift up)
sad	(*saed*)	miserable	(*miser*)
speed up	(*spōwan*=speed)	accelerate	(*accelerare*)
watch	(*waeccan*)	observe	(*observare*)
hate	(*hete*)	detest	(*detestari*)
do again	(*don*=do *ongēan*)	repeat	(*repetere*=try to get something back, revisit, repeat)

die	(*dēghen*)	expire	(*exspirare*=breathe one's last)
do well	(*don wel*)	succeed	(*succedere*)
hide	(*hȳdan*)	conceal	(*concelare*)
inner	(*innera*)	interior	(*interior*)

Write two paragraphs, telling the same story in each paragraph. In the first one, use at least five words or phrases from the first column. In the second paragraph, use at least five words or phrases from the second column. Begin the first one with 'The prince hid . . .', and the second with 'The prince concealed himself . . .'. See if you can keep the 'flavour' of each story consistent.

After you have finished, read each story aloud. Is one of the stories simpler than the other? Is one of them more pompous? Judging on style alone, which do you prefer?

Find a sentence on p.14 of this book which you think could be improved by using simpler words – and improve it.

N.B. (see p.49) Very many extremely common words in our language come from Latin. Use, cause, crime, beast, air, pen, pencil, table, animal, sock, sack, beer . . . The list could go on for a long time. We mustn't think that Latinate English is all 'fine writing'. English is like a magpie. It steals from many sources and keeps its liveliness.

To see the full richness of the English language at this stage, look at these three columns of words of similar meaning. The first consists of words descended from Old English, the second of words derived from Latin through French, and the third of words taken directly from Latin.

from Old English	from Latin via French	from Latin
fast	firm	secure
fire	flame	conflagration
fear	terror	trepidation
holy	sacred	consecrated

According to a historian of language, 'The difference in tone between the English and the French words is often slight; the Latin word is generally more bookish.' Do you agree?

In the fourteenth century, English started to be used in Parliament and the lawcourts (see time Chart, p.56). (We call the English of the Middle Ages Middle English.) English replaced Latin as the language in which lessons were taught in schools, though Latin remained the central subject in the curriculum. In the fifteenth century, written English became increasingly popular, although scholars still wrote in Latin. The last great English-speaking scientist to use Latin was Isaac Newton in his *Principia Mathematica* ('The Principles of Mathematics') published in 1687.

Can you think of any reasons why Newton may have chosen to write in Latin at this late date?

THE RENAISSANCE

Laocoon was a Trojan priest. He warned the Trojans not to take into their city the wooden horse which was left by the besieging Greeks. The gods, who wanted Troy to fall, sent two serpents to devour the priest and his two sons.

In 1506 this sculpture, which was made in about 50 B.C., was dug up on one of the hills of Rome, where it had lain hidden for a thousand years. Famous sculptors such as Michelangelo flocked to see it. This was typical of the surge of interest in the Ancient World at the time we call the Renaissance. The word means 're-birth'. Since the fall of the Roman Empire, the world of Greece and Rome had been glimpsed only in a kind of half-light. But now it was rediscovered in its full glory. As the word Renaissance tells us, it was as if it had been born anew.

One important result of the rediscovery of Roman civilization was that between 1500 and 1650 a new flood of Latinate words swelled the English language.

Here are seven of them: *benefit, consolidate, exert, exhilarated, exist, extinguish, mediate*. What do they mean?

C XXXIII.

Ludus Pilæ.

Tennis-Play.

In a Tennis-Court, 1. | In *Sphæriſterio*, 1.
they play | luditur
with a Ball, 2. | *Pilâ*, 2.
which one throweth, | quam alter mittit,
and another taketh, | alter excipit,
& ſendeth it back with | & remittit
· a Racket; 3. | *Reticulo*; 3.
and that is the ſport | idq; eſt Luſus
of Noble-men | Nobilium   (ris.)
to ſtir their body. | ad cõmotionem corpo-
   A winde-ball 4. | *Follis* (pila magna) 4.
being filled with air | aëre diſtenta
by a means of a Ventil, | ope *Epiſtomii*,
is toſſed to and fro | ſub dio
with the Fiſt 5. | *Pugno* 5.
in the open air. | reverberatur.

In a school book of 1659, students were taught how to play tennis in Latin. Note: at this time 's' could be written as 'f'.

This Latin takeover was strongly criticized. Some people contemptuously called the words from Latin 'inkhorn' words. What do you think they meant by this?

In the sixteenth and seventeenth centuries, many grammar schools were set up in England. Because all educated people employed in government or in business needed Latin, the schools' job was to teach it. Latin was in fact the basis of the education they provided.

The statutes of Oundle School in Northamptonshire (founded in 1556) required that all boys should speak Latin to each other 'as well in the school as coming and going to and from the same'. 100 years later, the charter of King James' Grammar School, Knaresborough in Yorkshire, was even more demanding. It stated that, after the first three years in the school, any boy caught using English, even in the playground, was to be beaten by the Headmaster!

Explain *either* why this strikes you as crazy *or* why it makes some sense to you.

At that time, all educated Europeans would have been able to speak Latin. This gave them an international language. Has any modern language begun to be adopted as an international language (for example, for air traffic control)?

So Latin entered the English language by four different routes.

43 A.D.	The Romans invade Britain.
597 A.D.	St Augustine comes to Britain.
1066 A.D.	The Normans invade Britain.
1500–1650 A.D.	The Renaissance in Britain.

DISCOS AND DICTIONARIES

A key moment in the development of the English language came in 1755 when Samuel Johnson published his great English Dictionary. Here is his definition of 'oats'.

OATS. *n. f.* [*aten*, Saxon.]   A grain, which in England is generally given to horfes, but in Scotland fupports the people.

It is of the grafs leaved tribe ; the flowers have no petals, and are difpofed in a loofe panicle : the grain is eatable. The meal makes tolerable good bread.   *Miller.*

The *oats* have eaten the horfes.   *Shakefpeare.*

It is bare mechanifm, no otherwife produced than the turning of a wild *oatbeard*, by the infinuation of the particles of moifture.   *Locke.*

For your lean cattle, fodder them with barley ftraw firft, and the *oat* ftraw laft.   *Mortimer's Hufbandry.*

His horfe's allowance of *oats* and beans, was greater than the journey required.   *Swift.*

Before Johnson spelling had been very free and easy. Shakespeare, for example, like everyone else of his time, had several ways of spelling his own name (Shakespere, Shakspear, Shakspere, Shagspere). Does it matter how we spell words?

After Johnson, spellings and meanings became standardized, though words often collected new meanings. Countless new words have entered the language since then. Many of these have been colloquial (belonging to the language of conversation).

Here are eight words from the *Oxford English Dictionary*: *punch-up, sleazy, chunder, hunky, splat, spaced out, zap, groupy*. Are there any that you would not have included in a dictionary? If so, why?

New words have often been coined to describe new sciences, inventions and discoveries. (See especially Unit 6.) Such words frequently come from Latin or Greek or a mongrel mixture of the two – for example: television, automobile, airport, appendicitis, vaccinate and disco.

The great seventeenth-century poet John Dryden wrote: 'I trade both with the living and the dead for the enrichment of our native tongue. We have enough in England to supply our necessity, but if we will have things of magnificence and splendour, we must get them by commerce.' What point is Dryden making with his metaphor of trade and commerce? Do you think that Dryden is right? Under what circumstances would *you* want to bring new words into the English language?

Some important facts

1. 340 million people in the UK, USA and the former British Empire speak English as their first language.
2. Another 300 million speak English as a second language. This figure includes some 34 million citizens of the USA whose first language is one of the 100 or more languages used for instruction in American schools.
3. In addition, there are many millions worldwide who learn English as a foreign language in school.

So you can see that English helped to spread a vast number of Latin words over a far wider area than they ever reached at the time of the Roman Empire.

4 · BUILDING ENGLISH FROM LATIN

We have inherited many things from the Romans and the most obvious of all, *if you know how to look for it*, is their contribution to our language. No other foreign nation has contributed so much.

Eight of the words in the above sentences come from Latin. Can you guess which they are?

Your address may be in a road or a lane (old English words). But it may be in a street, an avenue or a crescent – all words of Latin origin. You have already met the word 'street' (p.11); 'avenue' comes via French and means 'approach'; 'crescent' is pure Latin and means 'growing'.

What shape is a crescent moon? What has it to do with growing? What shape is a *croissant* (a French form of the same word)?

The flag of Pakistan includes a crescent, a Moslem symbol

a croissant

The Royal Crescent and The Circus at Bath, England

The easiest Latinate words to spot (and sometimes the hardest to understand) are those which end in *-tion* and *-sion* like 'contribution' above or 'diversion', which you may have seen on a road sign. They can have a rather alarming look, but if you learn how to take them to bits you will find they are not so alarming. The way will be open for you to understand not only hundreds of English words but plenty of words in French, Spanish, Italian – and some other languages too. The rest of this unit is about the bits.

See how many words you can make from the bits below. For each word, use one bit from column 1, one from column 2, and add *-ion* from column 3.

1	2	3
RE	CEPT	ION
EX	CLUS	ION
DE	STRUCT	ION
IN		ION
CON		ION

The bits in column 1 are called prefixes – bits fixed on the beginning. The bits in column 2 are called roots or stems, because they are the bits from which the meaning flowers. *-ion* in column 3 is a suffix, that is a bit fixed under or after.

Almost all *-ion* words have a Latin stem before *-ion*, and the stem always ends in *s* or *t*. Very many also have a prefix before the stem. You can see how the prefix affects the meaning of the stem by looking at *ex*clusion and *in*clusion. The meaning of the stem CLUS is 'shut'. What do *ex-* and *in-* mean?

Using a newspaper or book (this one, perhaps), spend some time making a collection, in alphabetical order, of as many words as you can find ending in *-tion* or *-sion*. Do this with attention, concentration and determination, but stop when suffering from constipation, dejection, depression, desperation, exasperation, exhaustion, indigestion, indignation, irritation or tension. (You can put these words in your list.)

Now look at the words 'desperation' and 'determination', 'exhaustion' and 'exasperation'. In each pair not only the endings but also the beginnings are the same. *de-* and *ex-* are prefixes you have met. Look at your list and see if you can find any further examples of prefixes shared by more than one word.

Prefixes

a *or* ab	*from*
ad	*to*
circum	*around*
con *or* co	*together*
contra	*against*
de	*down, from*
di *or* dis	*apart, in different directions*
e *or* ex	*out of*
in	*1. on, in, into*
	2. not
inter	*between*
ob	*in the way of*
per	*through*
pre	*in front of*
pro	*forward, forth*
re	*back, again*
se	*apart*
sub	*under, up under*
tra *or* trans	*across*

'dis' has also come to mean 'not' as in 'disagree'.

A word of warning is necessary about the prefix *in-*, which does two quite different jobs:

1 *in*clusion   **2** *in*digestion
   *in*vasion   *in*attention
   *in*scription   *in*visible

In Group 1 *in-* means 'in' or 'into' or 'on' (all more or less the same sort of meaning). In Group 2 *in-* means 'not'. Try to keep these groups separate in your list.

You can count as the same prefix, for example, *con-* in 'concentration', *col-* in 'collection', *cor-* in 'correction' and *com-* in 'competition'. The last letter of the prefix is changed to make the word easier to pronounce. Try saying *con*petition aloud and feel the struggle in your mouth. You are almost forced to say *com*petition. *ad-*, *in-*, *ob-* and *sub-* alter their last letter for the same reason. For example, *ad*-traction = attraction, *in*-mersion = immersion, *ob*-pression = oppression, *sub*-position = supposition.

Many stems have a little family of words around them, each with a different prefix. For example the following words are formed around the stem PRESS (which means 'press'!):

COM - PRESS - ION		OP - PRESS - ION
DE - PRESS - ION		RE - PRESS - ION
EX - PRESS - ION		SUP - PRESS - ION
IM - PRESS - ION		

See if you can find another family of words like this related to any of the words on your list. It may not be as big as the -PRESSION family. Try, for example, making a family round -JECTION.

Of course, as you will no doubt see from your list, many *-ion* words consist of just stem + ending, for example '*mot*-ion', '*miss*-ion', '*posit*-ion'. Sometimes a family gathers round such a word.

COM - MOT - ION

  DE - MOT - ION

    E - MOT - ION

PRO - MOT - ION

Collect two more families by adding different prefixes to -MISSION and -POSITION.

Here are some families in action. In the following sentences put in the prefix which makes sense:

1. The -*scription* on the tombstone was short.
2. He sent us a full -*scription* of his journey.
3. The doctor gave me a -*scription* for my cough.
4. The doctor gave me a flu -*jection*.
5. I have no -*jection* to your plan.
6. John has a happy -*pression* on his face, but his brother suffers from -*pression* and -*jection*.
7. That film made a great -*pression* on me.
8. -*mission* to the ground was by ticket only.
9. I had -*mission* to take a day off.
10. A new -*dition* of my book has been published.
11. In arithmetic I like -*dition* but -*traction* has no -*traction* for me.
12. It's a -*dition* in our family to have a package tour holiday every year.
13. I hope to get -*motion* to a higher class.
14. He did not show any -*motion* when his dog died.
15. The -*mission* of the movie was devoted to the noisy -*sumption* of popcorn.

Many of the stems from which these families of words are made describe some simple action with the hands. You have met for instance: PRESS (press), POSIT (place or put), MOT (move), MISS (let go), SCRIPT (write), JECT (throw), DIT (put or hand), CEPT (take), CLUS (shut), SUMPT (take), STRUCT (build), TRACT (pull).

What does the prefix do to the stem? Look at sentences 1 and 2 above: *in*scription means 'writing *on*'; *de*scription means 'writing *down*'. You can see that the prefix gives a special *direction* to the stem.

Write down the directions given by the prefixes in the other sentences above – some will be easy to describe, others quite difficult.

Now consider the ways in which we do the same sort of thing in our older, non-Latinate English idiom. We do use some prefixes, for example:
un as in 'undo', 'untie', 'uncover'
by as in 'bypass' (not quite the same as 'pass by')
over as in 'overtake' (not the same as 'take over') and 'overlook' (not the same as 'look over').
Can you give some examples to show how we use *out* and *under* as prefixes?

We also, with our magpie instinct, steal Latin prefixes and stick them on to English words – for example: subway, rebuild, pre-war, contraflow.

But the typical English way of twisting the meaning of verbs is by adding a word *after* the verb, as in 'take over', 'take up' and 'take down'. Look at these members of the 'put' family:

I was *put off* by his sneezing.

My interview has been *put off* till tomorrow.

We *put up* at a hotel.

We *put up with* the awful food.

You can see how English usually creates a family not by a prefix like Latin but by a word *after* the verb.

How many more examples of the 'put' family can you think of? Write some sentences to show how each is used. How many can you find in the 'take' family and the 'give' family? This will *take up* a lot of time. Don't *give up* or *give in* and don't be *taken in* by the simple look of English short words. Foreigners find them very difficult.

How would you explain to a foreigner the meaning of *up* in 'eat up', 'shut up', 'follow up'? Why do we shut *up* shop but close *down* a factory? Is there any difference between 'slow *down*' and 'slow *up*'? Why do we cut *down* a tree and then cut it *up*?

Just as these little English words after the verb give it a new twist of meaning, so the Latin prefixes give a twist to Latin verb stems. Sometimes the prefixes and stems have a quite straightforward meaning, but sometimes they don't.

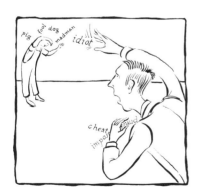

For instance in sentences 4, 5 and 6 on p.24, the stem JECT (throw) was used and the three words coming from this stem were: *injection, objection, dejection*. A doctor's *in*jection is something almost literally thrown *into* you by his needle. But an *ob*jection to your plan (something thrown *against* your plan or *in the way of* your plan) is not something *literally* thrown. Are we being literal when we say, 'He hurled insults at me'? And if I suffer from *de*jection (being thrown *down*), I am not literally thrown down, any more than if I say, 'I was really *thrown* when I heard I hadn't been picked for the team.' So look out for meanings which are not literal. Here are a few examples for you to try to explain. Use the table of prefixes on p.23.

PRESS is a stem meaning 'press'.

His footprints left an impression on the sand.

The film made a great impression on me.

What is different about the two uses of the word 'impression'?

CUSS is a stem meaning 'shake'.
  How do you explain: 1. concussion, and 2. discussion.

GEST is a stem meaning 'carry'.
  How do you explain: 1. digestion, and 2. suggestion.

LAT is another stem meaning 'carry'.
  How do you explain: 1. translation, and 2. elation.

MISS is a stem meaning 'let go'.
  Admission to the ground was free.
  By his own admission he eats too much.
  What is the connection between these two uses of the word
'admission'?

  What is the connection between 'promotion' and 'emotion'?

Look out too for a change of meaning in words as time goes by:
'aggravation' originally meant 'the adding of weight to'. (Where
else do you meet the stem *grav-*?) For example, 'The cold
weather led to the aggravation of his bronchitis.' But it has come
to mean the aggravation of anger in particular. So people say
'How aggravating!', meaning the same thing as 'How irritating!'

pre- + the stem VENT (*come*) make the words 'prevent' and
'prevention'. A church prayer begins 'Prevent us, O Lord, in all
our doings . . .' – which sounds to us as if it means 'Stop us,
O Lord, from doing anything'. But when it was first written it
meant simply 'Come in front of us, O Lord', meaning 'Protect us
like an advance-guard'.

We have chosen to look at *-ion* words because they are the easiest
to spot quickly. Round any *-ion* word in a dictionary there will
often be a cluster of other words. For example: *creation, creative,
creativity, creator, creature*, and of course *create*. Can you think of
a similar cluster round 'action'?

In these two groups the stem remains the same but has another
family – this time with different endings. What do you think the
suffix *-or* means? What is the equivalent non-Latinate ending?
What connection can you see between the meanings of the
following pairs of words?

motor	missile	fraction	native
motive	missionary	fracture	nature

Guess what the stems FRACT and NAT mean.

Now see how many words you can make using any prefix + any
stem mentioned so far + either of the suffixes *-or* or *-ive*.

Here is an extract from a dictionary with a typical collection of words gathering around one prefix and three stems from a single Latin verb. The prefix is *com-* and the stems POSIT, POS and PON:

compo[1] *kom'pō, n.* a mortar of cement: a mixture of whiting, resin, and glue for ornamenting walls and cornices: a bankrupt's composition: — *pl.* **com'pos.** [Abbrev. of **composition**.]

component *kem-pō'nent, adj.* making up: forming one of the elements or parts. — *n.* one of the parts or elements of which anything is made up, or into which it may be resolved. — *n.* **compōn'ency.** — *adjs.* **componental** (*kom-pō-nent'l*): **componential** (*-nen'shal*). [L. *com-pōn'ĕre.*]

compose *kem-pōz', v.t.* to form by putting together or being together: to set in order or at rest: to settle or soothe: to dispose artistically: to set up for printing: to create (esp. in literature and music). — *v.i.* to write (esp.) music: to set type. — *p.adj.* **composed'** settled: quiet: calm. — *adv.* **compōs'edly.** — *ns.* **compōs'edness; compōs'er** a writer or author, esp. of music: **composition** see **composite; composure** (*kem-pōzh'(y)er*) calmness: self-possession: tranquillity: composition: temperament, character (*Shak.*). [Fr. *composer* — L. *com-,* with, *pausāre,* to cease, rest; confused and blended in meaning with words from *pōnēre, positum,* to place.]

composite *kom'pe-zit,* formerly *-poz', adj.* made up of distinct parts of elements: — *ns.* **com'positeness; composi'tion** the act or art of composing: the nature or proportion of the ingredients of anything: a thing composed: a work of art, esp. in music: an exercise in writing prose or verse: disposition of parts: congruity: combination: an artificial mixture, esp. one used as a substitute: mental or moral make-up: a compromise: a percentage accepted by a bankrupt's creditors in lieu of full payment: a picture, photograph formed from several images: — *adjs.* **composi'tional; compositive** (*-poz'*). — *n.* **compos'itor** one who sets up type. — *adj.* **compos'itous** (*bot.*) composite. — *n.* **compost** (*kom'post*), **compŏst'ure** (*Shak.*) a mixture: a manure consisting of a mixture of decomposed organic substances. — *v.t.* **com'post** to treat with compost: to convert into compost. — *n.* **com'poster** an apparatus for converting garden waste into compost. — **composite portrait** a blend of several portraits: a photograph printed from several negatives representing different persons or the same person at different times; **composite resolution** a resolution or proposal made up from several similar resolutions and incorporating all their main points; **com'post-heap** a pile of plant refuse, soil, and often chemical fertiliser, which decomposes to form compost. [L. *compositus, compostus — com-,* together, *pōnēre,* to place.]

compot, compote *kom'pot,* or *kam'pōt, n.* fruit preserved in syrup: stewed fruit. [Fr. *compote;* cf. **composite**.]

compote, compotier. See **compot, comport**[2].

compound[1] *kem-pownd', v.t.* to make up: to combine: to settle or adjust by agreement: to agree for a consideration not to prosecute (a felony): to intensify, make worse or greater. — *v.t.* to agree, or come to terms: to bargain in the lump. — *adj.* (*kom'*) mixed or composed of a number of parts: in chem., resolvable into two or more elements, so united that the whole has properties of its own which are not necessarily those of its constituents, as in the case of a mixture: in arith., not simple, dealing with numbers of various denominations of quantity, etc., as in *compound addition,* etc., or with processes more complex than the simple process, as in *compound proportion.* — *n.* a mass made up of a number of parts: a word made up of two or more words: a compound substance (*chem.*) a compounded drug. — *n.* **compound interest** interest added to the principal at the end of each period (usu. a year) to form a new principal for the next period: **compound sentence** (*gram.*) one containing more than one principal clause; [O.Fr. *compundre* from L. *compōnēre — com-,* together, *pōnēre,* to place.]

a key to some of the abbreviations used in this dictionary **L.** = **Latin; Fr.** = **French; O.** = **Old.**

Make up five sentences each containing a different word from this page.

You will have noticed that if you knock the *-ion* bit off the end, you are often left with the verb in the family.

depression   to depress
subtraction   to subtract

But this is not always so.

admission   to admiss to admit
description   to descript to describe

There has been a small change of stem. This is because some Latin verbs had two stems – in this case MISS and MIT, SCRIPT and SCRIB.

deception   to decept   to deceive

Again there is a change of stem, this time because the word has come via the French *decevoir*.

What is the verb in the following families? *conclusion, procession, extension, expulsion, confusion, resolution.*

Second stems of Latin verbs produce little families of their own, with endings different from those we have so far considered. For example, CURR (a stem meaning 'run') produces 'occur', 'curr*ent*', 'curr*ency*', 'occurr*ence*', 'recurr*ent*'. How do you think these words come to mean what they do?

Take the stem FER (meaning 'carry' or 'bear') and see how many words you can make by adding different prefixes (see p.23). Try to show how the meaning of each word is explained by the meaning of the stem and the prefix. Then see how many further words you can make by adding *-ence* to the words you have made. What is the meaning of 'circumference'?

Note: Latin prefixes sometimes had the effect of altering the vowel in the stem, for example:

capt as in 'captive' becomes *cept* in 'receptive'.
fact as in 'factory' becomes *fect* in 'refectory'.

What does the stem *fact* mean? What is a refectory, and why is it so called?

5. HOW GREEK ENTERED ENGLISH

Look at the map (p.5). To the East of Italy lies Greece. Here there existed a civilization and a language older than those of Rome. (See Time Chart.) The ancient Greeks had a different alphabet which still survives today. In fact, modern Greeks still speak basically the same language as their ancestors.

Their alphabet was the first in which each letter stood for a single sound. Here it is:

Greek letter	name	English letter	sound
α	alpha	a	as in 'rat' or 'father'
β	beta	b	
γ	gamma	g	as in 'goose' (γγ = 'ng', γχ = 'nch')
δ	delta	d	
ε	epsilon	e	as in 'bet'
ζ	zeta	z	zd as in 'wisdom'
η	eta	e	as in 'there' (βη βη was the sound of a Greek sheep)
θ	theta	th	
ι	iota	i	as in 'bit' or 'machine'
κ	kappa	k or c	as in 'cat'
λ	lambda	l	
μ	mu	m	
ν	nu	n	
ξ	xi	x or ks	
ο	omicron	o	as in 'not'
π	pi	p	
ρ	rho	rh	
σ or ς	sigma	s	as in 'yes' (σ is used at the beginning or in the middle of a word, ς is used at the end.)
τ	tau	t	
υ	upsilon	u	as in French 'une', but it appears as *y* in English derivatives as in 'crypt'
φ	phi	ph	
χ	chi	ch	as in 'loch' or 'ro*ck h*ouse'
ψ	psi	ps	
ω	omega	o	as in 'sore'

΄ over a letter = h

Here are some Greek words for you to turn into English words: κωμα, κομμα, κωλον, κινημα, χαρακτηρ, βακτηρια, τραυμα, ἱπποποταμος, ῥινοκερως, αναλυσις.
What word do we get from the first two letters of the Greek alphabet? Capital δ (*delta*) was written Δ. What has this to do with the delta of a river?

Iota (the smallest letter) appears in English as 'jot' – as in the sentence 'I don't care one jot (or one iota) what you think'. What does this mean?

You may have met π in Mathematics – do you know what πr^2 is? You may also have met *gamma* rays in Science.

Who said, 'I am Alpha and Omega, the First and the Last'?

Greek letters originated from the Semitic language, where *aleph*, *beth* and *gimal* were *drawings* of an ox, a house and a camel! Semitic was the language spoken by the people who were supposed to be descended from Shem, the son of Noah – that is chiefly the Hebrews and the Arabs. The Hebrews and Arabs wrote from right to left. The Greeks, however, wrote from left to right, and it is from them that we get our custom of writing in this way.

Egyptian	Phoenician	Greek
ox's head	aleph	alpha
house	beth	beta
corner	gimmel	gamma

An illustration of the way Greek letters originated from drawings in Semitic languages.

For a long time, the Greeks did not have a written language at all. Homer, who lived before 700 B.C. and was the most famous of all their poets, did not write. He, and other poets like him, had to keep huge chunks of poetry in their heads. But soon after their time, the Phoenician alphabet, based on the Semitic alphabet, was adapted by the Greeks. Their new alphabet was to lead ultimately to the Roman alphabet – and so to all Western alphabets. A version of it provided the Russians with theirs.

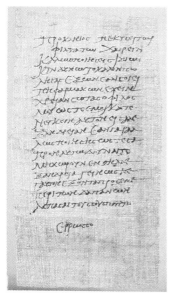

Papyrus letter

The influence of the Greek language on English has been entirely through books, not through speaking like Latin. For a long time, ancient Greek books were few, awkward to handle and liable to suffer quickly from wear and tear. They were made from a type of reed grown in the Nile delta by using thin strips of its pithy centre. The Greeks called it βιβλος or παπυρος.

Using the chart on p.29, change the Greek letters in these two words into English letters. Then say what English words are derived from the Greek words.

The strips of reed were glued together in a long roll. (Think of a roll of wallpaper or waxpaper.) The reader had to unroll it slowly from the right hand, holding in the left hand the part already read. The text, even if in verse, was written in narrow columns with no space between words and scarcely any punctuation. 100 pages of a small modern paperback would need a roll about 30 feet long and 10 inches high. Their ink was a mixture of soot and glue.

Make yourself a small imitation of a papyrus roll and write some English on it in the manner described, using capital letters. See how soon someone else can understand what you have written. Then write down all the disadvantages of such a book that you can think of.

It seems remarkable to us that books were ever written like this – perhaps even more remarkable that they were read. But it was in this form that the books which eventually influenced English thought and language were written. Most of these were written between 600 and 300 B.C. They include histories, poems, plays, philosophy, geometry and studies of nature. The New Testament, which was written in Greek, was compiled in the first century A.D.

Why do people write books nowadays? Do you suppose that writers in 500 B.C. felt the same motives?

It was not until about 200 A.D. that sturdier books began to replace papyrus rolls. They were made of parchment (animal skin) and arranged in leaves like a modern book. But they were still *manuscripts*. (What does '*man*uscript' mean? You know the stem 'script' already. What is a *man*icure? What is *man*ual labour? What is a gardening *man*ual? What do *man*age and *man*ufacture mean?)

The Greek and Roman books which we now possess survived almost entirely in the form of parchment manuscripts until parchment was replaced by paper in the tenth century and manuscripts by printing in the fifteenth century. The only other form of book used by Greeks and Romans was their equivalent of our writing-pad or exercise book. It consisted of one or more wooden tablets, coated with wax. Their writing-tool (*stilus* or *stylus*, from which we get our word 'style') was a small rod, sharp at one end for writing in the wax, blunt at the other for smoothing out. They used these tablets for anything from shopping lists or school exercises to love letters.

From left to right, some inkpots, a quill, a papyrus, two wooden writing tablets, and four pens.

Alexander the Great

What do you think would be the advantages and disadvantages of this manner of writing?

Knowledge of Greek books spread to the countries bordering the Eastern Mediterranean after a famous Greek king, Alexander the Great, conquered them in the fourth century B.C.

Greek books became widely known to the Romans when they conquered Greece in the second century B.C. By the next century, educated Romans could speak and write Greek. A Roman poet said, 'When Greece was taken captive, it captivated its barbarous conqueror.' What do you think he meant?

Through the Romans some second-hand knowledge of Greek history and thought filtered through to Britain, but very little knowledge of the Greek language. After the collapse of the Western part of the Roman Empire in the fifth century A.D. until the tenth century, Britain was cut off from any knowledge of Greek. But Greek influence came back to Europe by two routes:

1. via Spain. Greek books, mostly from the library at Alexandria in Egypt, had been translated into Arabic. The Moors from North Africa invaded Spain in 711 A.D. and as a result Arabic numbers and translations of Arabic books spread through Europe in the following centuries;

2. from Constantinople, which housed the other great library of Greek books. The Turks captured Constantinople in 1453 A.D. During the previous two centuries Greek scholars had travelled abroad with their books. With great enthusiasm, scholars in Europe set about learning the ancient Greek language and by the fifteenth century the way was open for Greek to influence the English language. This was a part of the great rebirth of knowledge which we call the Renaissance. (See p.17.)

6. THE GREEKS HAD A WORD FOR IT

The Greeks were the first to divide knowledge into different compartments. Many English words derived from Greek are especially concerned with special kinds of study or skill, for example subjects and skills taught in schools.

Write out the Greek words in column 1 below on a clean sheet of paper. Then make a second column, as in column 2 below, and write out the Greek word in column 1 in English letters. Then make a third column, as in column 3, and write the name of the school subject or skill:

1 Greek word and meaning	2 English spelling	3 School subject
ιστορια (*inquiry*)	historia	history
αριθμος (*number*)		
μαθηματα (*things learnt*)		
φυσικα (*things to do with nature*)		
μουσικα (*things to do with the arts*)		
δραμα (*something performed*)		
αθλητικα (*things to do with prizes*)		

Some subjects are derived from two Greek words. On a clean sheet of paper, write out the table below. Then in columns 2 and 4 write out in English letters the Greek words in columns 1 and 3. Then write the name of the subject which is made up from the two words.

1 Greek word and meaning	2 English spelling	3 Greek word and meaning	4 English spelling	5 School subject
γη (*earth*)	ge	γραφω (*write*)	grapho	geography
βιος (*life*)		λογος (*study*)		
τεχνη (*skill*)		λογος		
οικος (*house*)★		νομος (*system*)		

★Note: οι in Greek here becomes e in English

What subjects derive from γη + μετρον (*measure*)? γη + λογος (*study*)? What is the meaning of the word 'biography'? What Christian name does γη + ωργος (*worker*) produce?

The original telescope used by Sir Isaac Newton whose book *Principia Mathematica* was the last great English scientific work published in Latin.

Now look at the following words – all fairly new English words but all beginning with a very old Greek word (τηλε): *telephone, telegram, telegraph, telescope, telepathy, telephoto,* (*television, teleprinter*). The last two words are bracketed because *-vision* and *-printer* do not come from Greek. What does *tele-* mean? (Answer below.)

Here is a kit to explain these words. Write out the following list and put English spellings in the brackets:

List A

φων (phon) is a stem meaning 'voice' or 'sound'

γραμ (. . . . .) is a stem meaning 'something written'

γραφ (. . . . .) is a stem meaning 'write'

σκοπ (. . . . .) is a stem meaning 'look (at)'

παθ (. . . . .) is a stem meaning 'feel' or 'suffer'

φωτ (. . . . .) is a stem meaning 'light'.

Now explain the whole meaning of all the words beginning with *tele-*. What seems to be the literal meaning of 'photograph' and 'gramophone'?

From now on in this book, if you see (. . . . .) after a Greek word, write out the Greek word and its equivalent English letters in your exercise book.

tele- *means 'from afar'.*

35

Greek, like Latin, uses prefixes. Here are a few:

List B

δια (dia) meaning 'through' or 'between'
περι(. . . . .) 'around'
προ (. . . . .) 'before'
συν (. . . . .) or συμ (. . . . .) 'with'

Can you make any English words by putting a prefix from List B in front of a stem from List A? (Answers below[1].)

What is their literal meaning?

What words are produced by: 1. δια + μετρον, and 2. περι + μετρον? What do they mean?

The word 'period' comes from περι + όδος (*road, way*). Can you see how the word comes to have its present meanings?

Greek does not use only prefixes to make compound words. It has many more ways than Latin. It can add noun to noun, adjective to noun, etc. Take the stem λογ- which you have already met. It has a wide range of meanings, among which are 'speech', 'study', 'collection'.

1. What words can you make by adding the prefixes δια, προ and κατα (*down*) to the stem λογ-? How do you explain their meanings? First change the prefixes into English letters. (Answers below[2].)

2. What words can you make by adding the following before λογ?

Greek word and meaning	English spelling	English word (+ logy)	Meaning
θεος (*god*)	theos	theology	study of God or gods
ψυχη (*mind*)			
αρχαιος (*old*)			
αστρον (*star*)			
ανθος (*flower*)			

We make a distinction in English between *astronomy* and *astrology*. Do you know what it is? Can you see what an asterisk has to do with a star?

---

2. *dialogue, prologue, catalogue*

1. *diagram, periscope, program or programme, symphony, sympathy*

An astrological chart, showing the signs of the zodiac and the planets. Can you identify Scorpio, Libra and Cancer?

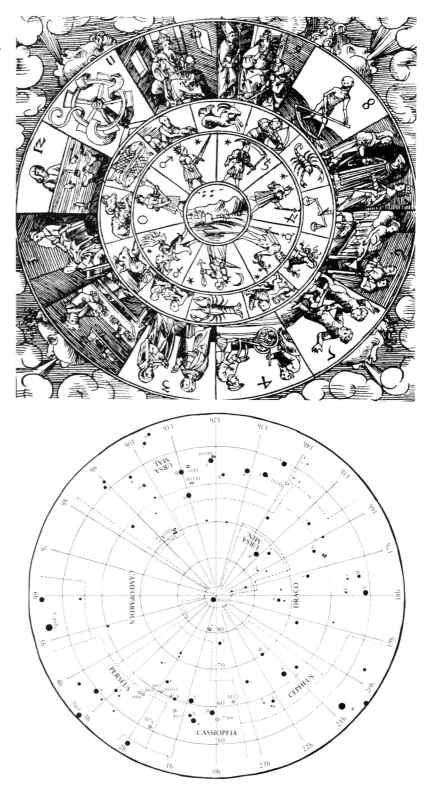

An astronomical chart, a guide to the night sky. What does Ursa mean? What do Maj. and Min. mean?

The word *doxology* means 'glory words' and is used especially to refer to the words at the end of every Christian psalm: 'Glory be to the Father . . .' The word *sockdolager* in the USA means 'a knock-out blow', 'a clincher'. Can you see any connection?

In the Greek alphabet o-μικρον means 'little o', ω-μεγα means 'big o'. Using List A, explain the meaning of: *microscope, microphone, megaphone*.

Can you suggest the derivation of the word 'microbe'? Where does the 'b' come from? (It comes from a Greek word you have met.)

GOVERNMENT

The Greek word πολις (. . . . .) meant a small state centring on a city. What English words are derived from this? (Answers below.[1])

The city of Naples was originally Νεα πολις (. . . . .), meaning 'new city'. What is a Neapolitan? Constantinople was originally Κωνσταντινουπολις (. . . . .), meaning 'the city of Constantine', who was Roman emperor in the fourth century A.D. It was the capital of the Eastern part of the Empire.

Can you think of one or two American cities with names ending in *-polis*? (Answers below.[2]) In the nineteenth century Manchester, England, was jokingly called Cottonopolis.

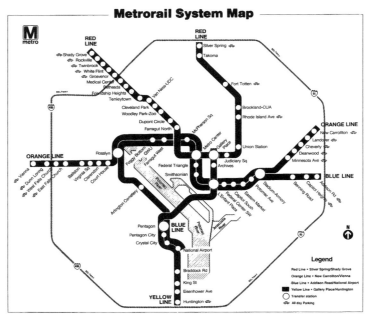

1. politics, policy, police   2. Indianapolis, Minneapolis

38

μητηρ (. . . . .) was the Greek word for mother. What is a *metropolis*? What does *metropolitan* mean? Why is the Metro in Paris and Washington, D.C. so called?

κρατ-	(. . . . .)	is a stem meaning 'power', from which we get the English -*cracy*
αρχ-	(. . . . .)	is a stem meaning 'rule', from which we get the English -*archy*
δημος	(. . . . .)	'people'
αριστος	(. . . . .)	'best'
ολιγος	(. . . . .)	'few'
μονος	(. . . . .)	'alone'
πλουτος	(. . . . .)	'wealth'

What words describing forms of government can you make by adding the words above to the stems κρατ- and αρχ-? What do the words mean?

The Greek word for bishop was επισκοπος (*overseer*). Why is an *arch*bishop so called?

In English we sometimes add Greek stems to un-Greek words: a main opponent is an — -*enemy*, rule by the squire is *squire*—.

Some of the words defining forms of government have an obvious meaning. But what about *aristocracy* and *democracy*? Who are 'the best' and who are 'the people'?

Among all peoples throughout history, there has been a tendency for the nobles to think that they are obviously the best people to govern, because they claim to be descended from kings. Hence the meaning of 'aristocracy' today. The Greeks were no exception.

The exact meaning of 'democracy' today is uncertain. What it meant to the Athenians of the sixth century B.C. who invented it was this. The population of Athens consisted of four main groups:

1. free-born native men
2. free-born native women and children
3. foreign residents of both sexes
4. slaves of both sexes (largely ex-prisoners of war).

Democracy meant power for the first group only. There was no president or prime minister of the modern type. All free-born men had the right to speak and vote in an open-air assembly and decide all matters of public policy by a majority verdict. Free-born women and foreigners had certain rights but slaves had none at all and were as much the possessions of their masters as a dog or a table.

The temples on the Athenian citadel, built at the high point of democracy in ancient Athens.

Have a discussion on the Athenian form of democracy. Was it fair? What skills were necessary among the free-born men to make the system work? In what sense could Britain or the USA or South Africa claim to be a democracy?

What do you think a δημαγωγος (. . . . . .) was? (αγ- is a stem meaning 'lead'.)

Most people who voted in the Athenian democracy could at least read. Greece was the first known example of such a democracy. In Ancient Egypt, only a few privileged people could read or write. Writing was called 'the speech of the gods'. In Greece, democracy and education went hand in hand. Do you think this must always be true? Why? Make a list of the ways in which education and the use of the citizen's vote are connected.

THE ARTS

Convert the following words into English lettering and you will quickly see what English words derive from them.

θεατρον (theatron) *watching-place*, τραγωδια (. . . . . .),
κωμωδια (. . . . .)
πο(ι)ημα (. . . . . .), πο(ι)ητης (. . . . .) *a maker*, επος
(. . . . . .), ελεγεια (. . . . .)

αρχιτεκτων (. . . . . .) *master-builder*
ωδη (. . . . . .) and μελος (. . . . . .) *song* or *tune*,
λυρικος (. . . . . .), ἁρμονια (. . . . . .), συμφωνια (. . . . . .),
ῥυθμος (. . . . . .), ὑμνος (. . . . . .), ψαλμος (. . . . . .),
ορχηστρα (. . . . . .), χορος (. . . . . .)

These last two words have changed in meaning over the years. ορχηστρα originally meant the area in the θεατρον where the small χορος (that is the small choir) *danced* and sang at various stages in a play. This area was originally on the same level as the actors. Later the word 'orchestra' came to mean the part of the concert hall assigned to the musicians, and the word 'chorus' to mean any large group of singers. But what does choreography mean?

The Greeks believed in the existence of nine Muses (Μουσαι), each of whom inspired a different art. Μουσειον meant a home of the Muses. What English word comes from it? What do you think an Odeon was originally?

What do the following words have in common?
λυρικος (. . . . . .), ωδειον (. . . . . .), αδελφοι (. . . . . .),
Απολλων (. . . . . .), κριτηριον (. . . . . .), ἱπποδρομια (. . . . . .),
Παλλαδιον (. . . . . .), φοινιξ (. . . . . .).

You may find the answer in the columns of a newspaper which advertise entertainments.

MEDICINE

Ancient Greek doctors, the most famous of whom is
Hippocrates, were quite good at διαγνωσις (. . . . .), that is in
knowing the nature of a disease, and at προγνωσις (. . . . .),
that is at predicting its progress. Until recently, doctors still took
the Hippocratic oath which bound them to treat their patients in
a conscientious and confidential manner. But his general theory
of how the body worked was odd, although it lasted into the age
of Shakespeare and beyond. Hippocrates thought that health
depended on the correct balance of four fluids or 'humours':
αἱμα (. . . . .) (*blood*), φλεγμα (. . . . .) (*phlegm*: thick fluid
from the nose or lungs), χολη (. . . . .) (*bile*), μελαινη χολη
(. . . . .) (*black bile*).

From αἱμα we get modern medical words such as *haemorrhage*,
haemophiliac, *haemoglobin* and *anaemic*. But the Latin word for
blood was *sanguis*, from which we get the word 'sanguine' –
which means 'having plenty of blood', hence 'optimistic'! From
φλεγμα comes 'phlegmatic' – which means 'having too much
phlegm', hence 'cool', 'unemotional'. From χολη comes
'choleric' – which means 'having too much bile', hence 'bad-
tempered'.

Can you say what too much 'black bile' was thought to lead to?
(Turn the Greek words into English letters.) (Answer below.)

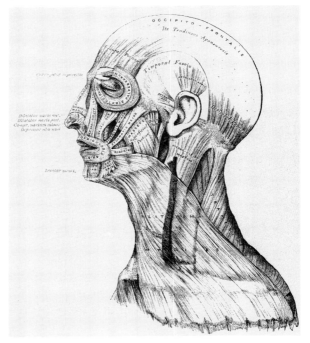

The human head, from the most
famous of medical books, Gray's
Anatomy, first published in 1858

melancholy

Despite these strange ideas, a very large number of modern medical terms comes from Greek. Here are a few:

1 Greek word and meaning		2 English spelling	3 English words
ασθμα	(*panting*)	asthma	asthma, asthmatic
πνευμονες	(*the lungs*)		
βρογχος	(*windpipe*)		
αρθρον	(*a joint*)		
δερμα	(*skin*)		
καταρρεω	(*flow down*)		
διαρρεω	(*flow through*)		
ανατομη	(*a cutting up*)		
ὑγιεινος	(*healthy*)		
αντι	(*against*) + βιος		
στηθος	(*chest*) + σκοπ		

Why is a pneumatic tyre so called? Where does a 'hypodermic' needle go? So what does ὑπο mean? Can you guess what the literal meaning of 'epidemic' is? (Remember δημος, p.39.) Guess what επι means.

βακτηρια (. . . . .) means 'sticks'; 'bacillus' in Latin means 'a little stick'. Can you explain the modern meanings?

◆

LOGIC

'Logic' is another word from λογος. It means the study of reasoning. The Greeks were pioneers in argument and methods of argument. Their cleverest men had a thirst for trying to answer such questions as 'What is a good man?', 'How do we know anything for certain?' The word for this activity was made up from:

φιλος (. . . . .) (*fond of*) σοφια (. . . . .) (*wisdom*). What is the English word which comes from these?

The stem φιλ- appears in several English words, for example
φιλ + ανθρωπος (. . . . .) (*human being*)
φιλ + λογος
βιβλιον (*book*) + φιλ
With the help of a dictionary find the English words and their meanings.

Imagine you are a philologist. Explain the meanings of *philharmonic, philately* (ατελεια means 'freedom from payment'), *Anglophile*. What first name comes from φιλ + ἱππος (. . . . .) (*horse*)?

SCIENCE

The Greeks did not contribute much to science as we know it. The word itself comes from the Latin *scientia* meaning 'knowledge' or 'skill'. But one of their answers to 'What is the world made of?' was ατομα (. . . . .) – α meaning 'not', τομα meaning 'splittable things'. In a word, what are these?

But the Greek language has been used for the making of many scientific and technical terms. Say what words we derive from:

δυναμις   (. . . . .) (*power*)

ηλεκτρον (. . . . .) (*amber*) See if you can discover the connection with amber.

ατμος   (. . . . .) (*vapour*) + σφαιρα (*globe*)

οζω   (. . . . .) (*have a scent or smell*)

φως   (. . . . .) (*light*) + φορος (. . . . .) (*carrying*)

ἑλικο   (. . . . .) (*spiral*) + πτερον (. . . . .) (*wing*)

Finally, several English words and expressions originate from ancient Greek names and places. Here are a few.

Αχιλλευς (. . . . .) was the hero of one of Homer's poems (see p.30). When he was young, his mother, a goddess, held him in the water of the River Styx, since this was supposed to be a complete protection against wounds. But she had to hold him by the heel. He was eventually killed by an arrow in the heel. Athletes often damage their Achilles tendon. Where is it? What would a teacher mean by saying, 'Arithmetic is your Achilles' heel'?

Ολυμπια (. . . . .) is the name of a place in Southern Greece where competitions in running, boxing and other sporting activities were held every four years from 776 B.C. to 393 A.D. Similar competitions were revived in 1896 and have continued since then every four years. What are they called?

Look back at the meaning of athletics (p.34). Now suggest what *pentathlon* and *decathlon* mean. (πεντε means 'five', δεκα means 'ten'.) γωνια means 'angle'. So what is a *pentagon*? What is the Pentagon and why is it so called?

Μαραθων (. . . . .) is the name of a place north east of Athens where the Athenians fought against a Persian invasion army in 490 B.C. The story goes that an Athenian runner – who had already run 150 miles in two days to spread the news of the

The Pentagon in Washington D.C. What happens here?

invasion – fought in the victorious battle against the Persians, ran back to Athens (a distance of about 26 miles) to report the victory and then died. By what modern race is he remembered?

Television stations sometimes broadcast a Telethon. What is it?

One of the world's most famous running shoes is called after the Greek word νικη (. . . . .) meaning 'victory'.

The Nike Air Max Light.

7. LATIN GRAMMAR AND ENGLISH – SAME OR DIFFERENT?

Pippa is eating ice cream.

The **verb** in a sentence tells us what is happening. So what is the verb in the sentence above? Who is doing the eating? How can you tell? We call the *doer*, the person who is performing the action of the sentence, the **subject**.

You will see that 'ice cream' is left over. What in this sentence is *affected* by the action of the verb and has something *done to* it? It's the ice cream, of course, which starts off in a bowl but ends up inside Pippa. What words can you suggest to describe the person or thing in a sentence that has something done to it? For example, would 'victim' be a good word? The traditional name for this is the **object** (which means 'something thrown in the way'). Do you think this is a better word than any of those you have thought up?

What is the subject and what is the object in the following sentences?

The referee blew the whistle.

The striker scored a penalty.

The Beatles played gigs all over the world.

David Bowie's groupies kept hounding him.

In English, the order of the words usually tells us what is the subject and what is the object. 'Agassi beat Edberg' and 'Caesar beat Pompey' are very different from 'Edberg beat Agassi' and 'Pompey beat Caesar'. Latin on the other hand shows the difference by changing the endings of its words. The object ends in *m*. So *servus* ('slave') will be the subject while *servum* will be the object.

dominus servum spectat.   'The master looks at the slave.'

What is the Latin word for 'looks at'?

So in Latin the different endings show us the different jobs the words have to do in the sentence. The order the words come in doesn't basically alter what they are saying. For example: *servum dominus spectat* still means 'The master looks at the slave'. But it puts the emphasis on the word *servum* – it's the *slave* that the master is looking at.

We have names for the various jobs which nouns perform in a Latin sentence. We call them 'cases', and you will need to know this word if you learn German, Greek or Russian.

The *nominative* case is the case of the subject.

The *vocative* case is the case by which you address someone (for example, 'Be careful, *dad*!').

The *accusative* case is the case of the object.

The *genitive* case means 'of'.

The *dative* case means 'to' or 'for'.

The *ablative* case means 'by', 'with', 'from', 'at', 'in' or 'on'.

Here are the different cases of *servus*:

nominative	servus
vocative	serve (two syllables)
accusative	servum
genitive	servi
dative	servo
ablative	servo

Change the words in italics into Latin:

the job *of the slave*

I hit *the slave*.

I gave a rabbit *to the slave*.

We still have some different case endings in English.

The master saw the girl working. *He* praised *her*.

He is the subject and therefore in the nominative; *her* is the object and therefore in the accusative. Fill in the gaps in these sentences:

The girl sees her mother. — calls —.

The mother is looking for her son. — cannot find —.

We are lost. Can our parents find —?

In what cases are *she, him, her, we, whom, he* and *us*?

Discuss the following sentences. If you were teaching English, what comments would you make on the words in italics.

She took dad and *I* out to lunch.

That is the teacher *who* I don't like.

Her and *him* were out at the pub when it happened.

Us couldn't care less!

Thee I wed.

While it is certainly true that Latin words alter much more than English ones to show what job they are doing in a sentence, many English verbs change quite dramatically in their past tenses:

for example, *I flee — I fled*. What is the past tense of: *see, sit, spit, flit, seek, buy, do, make*?

One more point. In English we usually make a word 'plural' (from the Latin *plures* meaning 'more') by adding an *s* to it – for example *apple* = singular, but *apples* = plural. But when we are dealing with Latin and Greek words which have become part of the English language we have to use Latin and Greek plurals. Look at the following:

singular	plural
phenomenon	phenomena
criterion	criteria
datum	data
medium	media
radius	radii

Find out the plural of *hippopotamus*, *index* and *formula*.

When Latin was spoken in the ancient world, it changed and developed as any modern language does. However, only a certain number of Latin texts have survived from the golden age of Latin literature. From these we can work out a number of clear grammatical rules which were almost always obeyed. So we can generally say what was right and wrong in Latin.

With living and rapidly changing languages like our own, we can't have many rules of this kind. Often, all we can do is describe how the language is used at a particular time. So be on your guard when people tell you that something in English is ungrammatical. They may just mean that they are not accustomed to it!

'Who is that?' 'It's him.' This is good English usage. In Latin, however, it would be wrong. You would have to say 'It is he.' You must not try to apply the rules of Latin grammar to English.

In the fifteenth century A.D., the Holy Roman Emperor Sigismund, who was a German, once made a grammatical mistake in his Latin. When told of this, he replied, 'Ego sum Imperator Romanorum, et supra grammaticam.' (He got his grammar right this time!) What do you think this means? (Answer below.)

I am the Roman Emperor and above grammar.

8. ET CETERA

In this final unit we show various ways in which Latin and Greek are still alive today. Our title *et cetera* means 'and the rest', 'and so on' in Latin, and is usually shortened to **etc**. Other useful Latin expressions of this kind are:

i.e.   *id est* meaning 'that is', 'that is to say'

e.g.   *exempli gratia* meaning 'for example'

a.m.   *ante meridiem* meaning 'before noon'

p.m.   *post meridiem* meaning 'after noon'

P.S.   *Post Scriptum* a 'postscript', i.e. 'something written later'

A.D.   *Anno Domini* meaning 'in the year of our Lord'
(In what cases are these two Latin words? see p.47)

N.B.   *Nota Bene* meaning 'Note well'

v.   *versus* meaning 'against'

Think up nine sentences, using one of these expressions in each.

◆

Here are some questions:

1. Ceres was the Roman goddess of corn. Why would you think of her at breakfast?

2. *Calculus* is the Latin word for 'a pebble'. Suggest how the meaning of 'calculate' is connected with the Latin word.

3. *Orient* means 'rising'. Where is the Orient and why is it so called? Where is the *Occident* (this means 'falling')?

4. The Latin word for 'island' is *insula*; the Italian word is *isola*. How many English words can you find that come from these stems?

5. a) 'Fact' is derived from Latin *factum*, meaning 'something done'.
   b) 'Fate' is derived from Latin *fatum*, meaning 'something spoken'.
   c) 'Date' is derived from Latin *datum*, meaning 'something given'.

   How do you explain the last two? N.B. on (c): Rome had no Post Office.

6. The Latin *panis* survives in pantry, companion, French *pain*, Spanish *pan* and Italian *pane*. What used to be kept in the pantry? What did 'companion' originally mean?

7. *Tandem* is Latin for 'at last' or 'at length'. Can you see how we have come to speak of a bicycle for two as a 'tandem' bicycle?

8. *Fac simile* is Latin for 'make a copy'. What machine derives its name from these words?

◆

CLASSICAL NAMES

Here is something which you may find useful when you are reading stories from classical mythology. Greek has come down to us filtered through Latin. So Greek gods and heroes tend to be known to us by their Latin names (or at any rate names based on the Latin).

Write out the English names for the following. If you are in doubt about any of them, you can probably find a dictionary which will give you the answer. (H is capital η.)

Greek name		Latin name	English name
Αχιλλευς	(. . . . . .)	Achilles	Achilles
Οδυσσευς	(. . . . . .)	Ulixes	
Μενελαος	(. . . . . .)	Menelaus	
Ἑλενη	(. . . . . .)	Helena	
Πριαμος	(. . . . . .)	Priamus	
Ἑκαβη	(. . . . . .)	Hecuba	
Ζευς	(. . . . . .)	Juppiter	
Ἑρμης	(. . . . . .)	Mercurius	
Αφροδιτη	(. . . . . .)	Venus	
Ἡφαιστος	(. . . . . .)	Vulcanus	
Αρτεμις	(. . . . . .)	Diana	
Ἡρα	(. . . . . .)	Juno	
Δημητηρ	(. . . . . .)	Ceres	
Περσεφονη	(. . . . . .)	Proserpina	
Αθηνα	(. . . . . .)	Minerva	
Αρης	(. . . . . .)	Mars	
Ἑστια	(. . . . . .)	Vesta	
Απολλων	(. . . . . .)	Apollo	

Paris was a Trojan prince who had to award a golden apple to the most beautiful of three goddesses. Who were these three goddesses, and what disaster resulted from Paris's decision?

Here is a story in which the words in italics are all unchanged in form and spelling from the original Latin:

Samuel Smith, *alias* Slippery Sam, was in action again, and by order of the Prime *Minister* police were called in from a large *radius* around London. But at the crucial moment, a police *camera* went out of *focus*. Smith would have had no *alibi* if the photo had come out. As it was, he led the police a proper *caper* and finally jumped on an *omnibus* and escaped. This was an *extra* worry for the P.M., especially as the *media* headlined the story and called the whole thing a *recipe* for chaos.

The Latin meaning of the words in italics is:

alias	at other times	*alibi*	elsewhere
minister	servant	*caper*	a goat
radius	rod or spoke	*omnibus*	for all
camera	a vaulted arch or chamber	*extra*	outside
		media	things in the middle
focus	a hearth or fireside	*recipe*	take! (an instruction)

How do you explain the English use of these words?

Say what is meant by the words in italics in the following sentences. You can use a dictionary. They are all Latin, apart from the two in 7 which are Greek.

1. If you give me the *data* I need, I'm happy to work this out on my computer.
2. Can you tell me the *agenda* for the Stamp Club's meeting after lunch today?
3. Do you think that Beethoven's Ninth Symphony is his *magnum opus*?
4. I am not completely happy about the circumstances of her death. There will have to be a *post mortem*. Meanwhile the matter is *sub judice*.
5. The dreadful news left me completely *nonplussed*.
6. *Exeunt omnes* (via the *exit*).
7. You have noted a very strange *phenomenon*. What are the *criteria* by which you are judging?
8. The witness wishes to remain *incognito* and so the judge is hearing the case *in camera*.

INSCRIPTIONS, COINS AND MOTTOES

Lapis is Latin for 'a stone'. (With your knowledge of prefixes, can you see the literal meaning of 'dilapidated'?) Latin has been called a 'lapidary' language, i.e. particularly suitable for use on monuments, tombstones, etc. Why? Because Latin often takes fewer letters and less space to say something than English does. (Letters and space on stone both cost money.)

For a start Latin differs from all major European languages except Russian in not having any word for 'a' or 'the'. In other ways, too, it is economical. Take, for instance, the Latin saying *in vino veritas*, which means literally, 'in wine the truth' – i.e. the more wine you drink, the more likely you are to say what you really think. See who can find the shortest way of expressing this idea in natural English.

Shortage of space is an obvious problem with coins. Take a coin out of your pocket and look at the 'heads' side. If you are British or Canadian, you'll see the head of the Queen. To the left of this head you will read D.G.REG.F.D. This is short for DEI GRATIA REGINA FIDEI DEFENSOR. It is Latin and it means 'By the Grace of God, Queen and Defender of the Faith'. Find out why since Henry VIII (1491–1547) every monarch of England has been called FIDEI DEFENSOR. It is an interesting story.

F.D. does not appear on Canadian coins. Why? Have a look at some pound coins. You'll find that around the edge of these there is an inscription. This varies. See how many different inscriptions you can discover. What language are these inscriptions in, and what do they mean?

In the USA the penny, nickel, dime and quarter have E PLURIBUS UNUM on the reverse. What does this mean? (Answer below.)

Scottish and English pound coins have Latin inscriptions:
  NEMO ME IMPUNE LACESSIT No one harms me without being punished. (Scottish).
  DECUS ET TUTAMEN Our ornament and protection. (English).
Welsh pound coins have a Welsh inscription:
  PLEIDIOL WYF I'M GWLAD I support my country.
The Scots also use paper notes.

◆ ───

ROMAN NUMBERS

Now look on the right hand side of the Queen. You will see her name, Elizabeth II. What does the II bit mean? It's the Roman number 2. In English we use Arabic numbers almost all of the time (see p.33 for the influence of the Arabic civilization on our own). But sometimes, as on these coins, you will meet Roman numbers.

a union from many states.

52

Here are the Roman numbers from 1 to 10:

1	I	6	VI
2	II	7	VII
3	III	8	VIII
4	IIII or IV	9	IX
5	V	10	X

They work like this: I = 1; if you want to make that 2, you add another I; the same goes for 3 which is III. For 4, you can write IIII. But there is another way of writing 4: the Roman number 5 is V, and if you put I *in front of* V, you show that you want to subtract the I and not add it on. So 4 can be IV, while 6 is VI.

1. The Roman number 10 is X. What are the Roman numbers for 11, and 15?
2. The Roman number 20 is XX. What are the Roman numbers for 19 and 30?
3. The Roman number 50 is L. What are the Roman numbers for 40, 49, 60, 61?
4. The Roman number 100 is C, 500 is D and 1,000 is M. What year is MCMLXXXIV?

Next time you watch an old film, look at the credits and see if you can spot the date the film was made. Copy it down quickly and work out what year it is.

Here are some more questions:

1. *Meander* was the Greek name of a river in Turkey (now called Menderes). What sort of river is it?
2. *Planetes* in Greek meant 'a wanderer'. Why is a *planet* so called?
3. *Chronos* is Greek for 'time'. How do you explain the meaning of *chronometer, chronicle, chronic*?
4. The Arctic Ocean derives from the Greek *arctos* meaning 'a bear'. How do you explain this? (The Greeks had never met polar bears, but they studied the stars.)
5. The Greek word *cosmos* first of all meant 'order' or 'arrangement', then 'the universe', then 'the world'. Which meanings does it have in the English words *cosmopolitan, cosmonaut, cosmetics*?

MORE ABOUT POLITICS

Here in alphabetical order are some Latin words and stems, from which the names of various political parties in Britain, USA and elsewhere are derived:

communis	in common
labor	work
liber	free
radix	root
respublica	the state (literally 'the public thing')
-servat-	is a stem meaning 'keep'
socius	a partner

Name the parties and say why you think they chose their names.

Here are the Latin stems from which important elements in the American constitution are named:

-SID- is a stem meaning 'sit'

-GRESS- is a stem meaning 'walk'

-SEN- is a stem meaning 'old' (as in *sen*ior citizen)

What are the words formed from these stems, and what is their literal meaning?

P.S. The US Congress meets on Capitol Hill. Where is the original Capitol Hill?

---◆---

Choose three of the following words, and, using an encyclopedia and a dictionary, write out: (a) the story behind the words, and (b) the meaning of the words in English:

1. You can bestride the narrow world like a *colossus*.
2. You can *hector* your opponent.
3. You can undertake a *Herculean* labour.
4. You are *Narcissistic* if you like looking in the mirror.
5. You can set out on an *Odyssey*.
6. You can be strangled by a *python*.
7. You can show *Spartan* fortitude.
8. You can *tantalize* your victim.
9. You can be a *titanic* figure or sink like the *Titanic*.

GREEK ANIMAL NOISES

Below is a list of Greek words representing the noises made by various animals.

dog	αυ
cow	μυ
frog	βρεκεκεκεξ
lamb	βη βη
dolphin	μιμυ
owl	κικκαβαυ
cuckoo	κοκκυ

See how many English words you can find for animal noises. What words are used in other modern languages?

If you wanted to scare away birds in Ancient Greece, you would say σου σου. What do we say today?

Think about all these sounds and then guess why the Greeks called people who didn't speak Greek 'barbarians'. (Hint: barbar. Compare our phrase 'mumbo jumbo'.)

TIME CHART

B.C. = Before Christ
A.D. = Anno Domini (meaning 'in the year of our Lord' – i.e. after the birth of Christ.)
   c. = circa (meaning 'around')

B.C.

c.1750	The Semitic alphabet comes into existence
776	The first Olympic Games
753	Legendary date of the founding of Rome by Romulus
c.750	Homer's poems, the Iliad and the Odyssey, in Greek Writing comes to Greece
500–400	The Golden Age of Athenian democracy
323	Death of Alexander the Great
200–100	Rome extends its power into the Mediterranean
146	Greece becomes part of the Roman Empire
55 & 54	Julius Caesar raids Britain
c.4	Birth of Christ

A.D.

43	The Romans conquer Britain
122	Hadrian's Wall built
328	Constantinople becomes the capital of the Eastern part of the Roman Empire
410	The Romans leave Britain The Western Roman Empire collapses
400–600	The Saxons, Jutes and Angles invade Britain bringing the Anglo-Saxon language with them
597	St Augustine brings a new wave of Christianity to Britain
711	The Moors invade Spain bringing their Arabic translations of Greek books
1066	The Normans invade Britain, bringing Norman French with them
1362	Statute of Pleading: all lawsuits to be conducted in English instead of French
1453	The Turks sack Constantinople
1475	Caxton prints the first book in English
1492	Columbus crosses the Atlantic and begins the colonization of the Americas
1616	Death of Shakespeare
1687	Isaac Newton's *Principia Mathematica* published, the last great scientific work in Latin by an English scientist
1755	Samuel Johnson's dictionary published